God's Loud Hand

Also by Kelly Cherry

God's
Loud
Hand

Poems by Kelly Cherry

Louisiana State University Press
Baton Rouge and London
1993

Library of Congress Cataloging-in-Publication Data
Cherry, Kelly.
    God's loud hand : poems / by Kelly Cherry.
      p. cm.
    ISBN 0-8071-1820-6 (cloth). — ISBN 0-8071-1821-4 (pbk.)
    I. Title.
    PS3553.H357G63   1993
    811'.54—dc20   92-37037
                                        CIP

Grateful acknowledgment is made to the publications in which the following poems first appeared, sometimes in different versions or under different titles:

    America: "And Then"; *Anglican Theological Review:* "In the Garden by the Sea: Easter," "The Island of Contentment," "Song About the Second Creation"; *Appalachian Journal:* "Air on Air," "Lullaby," "Song of the Dreaming Geologist"; *Bloodroot:* "Appoggiatura"; *Caprice:* "The Same Rose"; *Crazy Horse:* "Song About Creation," "Song of the Wonderful Surprise"; *Denver Quarterly:* "Love"; *Four Quarters:* "Song of Despair," "Body Song," "Song of the Housewife"; *Gettysburg Review:* "Green That Inspires Longings for Joy"; *Hollins Critic:* "Song with Footnote"; *Literatūra un Māksla* (in translation by Viktor Kalnin; Latvia): "Air on Air," "Aubade," "Song of the Farmer"; *Lullwater Review:* "The Blossoming"; *Midwest Quarterly:* "In the End"; *New Letters:* "Berlin: An Epithalamion"; *New Literary History:* "Now the Night" (as part of an essay); *Open Places:* "Reading, Dreaming, Hiding"; *The Pilot:* "Song of Remembering"; *Richmond Literature and History Quarterly:* "Song About Being Without Him," "Song for One World," "Song of Need and Desolation," "Song of Time"; *River Styx:* "Grammaire Générale: A Review"; *Shenandoah:* "The Promise," "The Name"; *Southern Poetry Review:* "Galilee"; *Techu Wenxue* (in translation by Yeh Chun-chan; People's Republic of China): "Air on Air," "Song of Remembering," "Lullaby"; *Yarrow:* "Report from an Unnamed City."

    "Gethsemane" © 1988 Kelly Cherry, as first published in *The Atlantic.* "Grace" © 1990 Kelly Cherry, as first published in *The Atlantic.* "History" and "Prayer" were first published by the Phi Beta Kappa Society in the *American Scholar.*

    "Love" was reprinted in *Contemporary Religious Poetry,* ed. Paul Ramsey (New York, N.Y., and Mahweh, N.J.: Paulist Press, 1987).

    The cycle *Songs for a Soviet Composer* was published as a chapbook by Singing Wind Press (St. Louis, 1980). These songs were written as a text for the Latvian composer Imant Kalnin; therefore, for readers rightly cognizant of the continuing legal independence of the Baltic nations since 1918, the preferable title might have been "Songs for a Latvian Composer." I have used the word "Soviet" to emphasize Latvia's status, at the time of the cycle's composition, as an occupied country, a fact that is central to an understanding of the relationship the songs portray. For his sensitive translation of the complete cycle into Latvian, which first appeared in *Karogs* (Riga, 1992), I am indebted to Valters Nollendorfs.

    The quoted line from "Readings" by Czeslaw Milosz is translated by him and Lillian Vallee (*Bells in Winter;* New York: Ecco Press, 1978).

    Heartfelt thanks go also to the Virginia Center for the Creative Arts and the Corporation of Yaddo.

Publication of this book has been supported by a grant from the National Endowment for the Arts in Washington, D.C., a federal agency.

Contents

IV   *A Joyful Noise*

I *Common Prayers*

It is a thing plainly repugnant to the Word of God, and the custom of the primitive Church, to have publick Prayer in the Church, or to minister the Sacraments in a tongue not understanded of the people.

—*The Book of Common Prayer*

[E]xcept ye utter by the tongue words easy to be understood, how shall it be known what is spoken? for ye shall speak into the air.

There are, it may be, so many kinds of voices in the world, and none of them is without signification. . . .

Wherefore let him that speaketh in an unknown tongue pray that he may interpret.

For if I pray in an unknown tongue, my spirit prayeth, but my understanding is unfruitful.

What is it then? I will pray with the spirit, and I will pray with the understanding also: I will sing with the spirit, and I will sing with the understanding also.

—1 Corinthians 14: 9–10, 13–15

Galilee

Suppose another time while walking on water
he grew weary and decided to sit down
upon a wave cresting in a white curve
under the sun, to catch his breath, and fish
swam back and forth around him, silver needles
sewing the sea in a seamless stitchery,
the sun a sequin on the bright bodice of sky,
the anchoring hem of his robe embroidered with salt.

You on the shore! Can you imagine how
you would have felt, knowing that here was a god
at sea, one who had already gotten
his feet wet, one who, though he was not in
over his head, was drifting even then
toward the nakedness of eternity?

The Radical

Think of it: the master a servant.
Getting down on his knees,
washing the feet,
the Achilles' heels and calloused soles,
the secret, shamed places between the toes.

Not the symbolic swipe we see in the movies.
No, the towel getting filthier and filthier, after all the walking
they had done, and perhaps
the weather was not always so good
it had rained, there had been mud
it had not rained, it was extremely hot,
so hot they didn't even piss, residue of salt on their skin so thick
it was nearly geological,
as they crossed from Bethany into Jerusalem
and mixed in the crowded, urgent streets of the city,

which was palmy with spangled sunlight,
bright coins scattered on the buildings' sides.

So much yet to happen! And yet it would happen
and be over seemingly before it had begun,
the way life is,
the way we arrive at our single destination
before we have quite packed,
the bits and pieces of our experience exposed to anyone,
which means that the future is constantly revealing itself as having been
the past all along,

which means that time returns us to ourselves.

(Even if you *thought* you were moving away from yourself,
thought you could outpace that peculiar dialectic . . .)

And now he traces each instep with the nap of the towel
as if it were a country he wants to map,

4

as if he wants to remember where it has been,
the steps it took
to get here,

the earth it walked on—
to him, a miracle greater than walking on water.

Gethsemane

On a hill backlit by twilight,
the disciples gather like crows
for the night.

This is their down time, time to browse
among the olive branches, Christ with them,
their apostolic flight slowed at last to a head-nodding drowse,

to a flutter of tattered cloak, the unraveling hem
dragging in the dirt like a hurt wing.
They flock momentarily around him,

then settle down, safe in the soft swing
of wind that rises and then falls back
with the deepening evening

into the distance, and sleep, while Christ's black
feathers burn in his father's fist,
plucked by God before by Judas kissed.

Golgotha

And when they were come unto a place called Golgotha, that is to say,
a place of a skull . . .
                                                          —Matthew 27:33

"Et uenerunt in locum qui dicitur Golgotha, quod est Caluariae
locus." . . . Ex quo apparet Caluariae . . . locum significare decollato-
rum, ut ubi abundauit peccatum superabundet gratia ["And they came
to a place called Golgotha, where Calvary is." . . . Therefore the name
of Calvary appears . . . to signify "a place of the decapitated," so that
where sin has abounded grace may be superabundant].
                                      —Jerome, *Commentary on St. Matthew*

They were scattered on the hillside like stones,
polished by the wind-rag: the smooth, shining bones,
cheekbone and eye socket, the empty skull-cases

of brains that had vanished into various gullets, leaving no traces
of thought, not even a single, stray
idea. For much of that long, painful day

he must have contemplated the meanings of
erosion, mortal decay, vanity, impermanence, rather than love,
until in the lengthening light

that drew on toward—but he would never see it—that night,
he saw—a trick of his blood-blurred eyes, perhaps—them move,
and knew the meaning of the skulls was love

and knew the one proposition needing no proof
is that God exists because God thinks or is thought of.
God is what remains in the final analysis.

The Blossoming

The centurion speaks

Too green and sweet for them to think of standing guard in,
That place we plucked him from, rose in the garden.

Call it the botany of betrayal.
We transplanted him to this barren hill,

Never dreaming he could grow on a cross.
He was like a ruined rose,

The long stem of his body bent at the knees—
And the tears of the onlookers on their knees

Fell to the ground, watering it with love,
Until time itself flowered into the fullness of.

The Same Rose

For so long we kept trying to
kill the divine in ourselves
with every possible instrument of destruction,
tangible and intangible,
but the divine kept resurrecting itself
quite in spite of us
(a species blind to the numinous),
so that it began to seem as if
grief and triumph were one and perennial,
petals on the same rose,
or the same rose by other names.

Reasons

Woman, why weepest thou?
—John 20:13

Because he was the best part of myself and has gone, leaving me
    with the least part of myself,
Because with his departure, the rose has become a rose merely,
    beautiful but finite,
Because in his absence, earth has become the address of his
    absence, the place where he is gone from,

And so the rose, beautiful and finite, is also haunted by its memory
    of itself and is both what it is and the loss of what it was,
And so my heart, too, is finite, bounded on all sides by an
    emptiness so immense that it is like a desert wilderness,

Which is what the garden, so deceptively green and bright,
    really is,
Which is what the sky, asleep in its private dream for centuries
    now, really is,

And our entire, hurting earth has become a ruining garden in
    which the roses, once rampant as life, are like blotches of
    blood, a scarlet fever,
A still-weeping sore, my heart, which love had made an oasis,
A mirage, my self
A mirage, this cool blossoming of watery tears

Eternal and unreal. . . .

In the Garden by the Sea: Easter

These giant grape hyacinths
Rise like porticoes from stems like plinths,
Flinging their fragrance

On the April air.
Something *is* everywhere,
Something like air

Or God, is there where you thought
There was nothing, not
Anything, where matter, caught

And stuck
On a hook,
Squirms and is eaten, solider than any book

A writer ever wrote.
Something exists that is not merely of note,
Something unwritten but wrought

In sense and dimension,
Something like an ocean,
Say, or the moment of bright tension

Before the body gives
Itself to the idea that it lives
And is loved and loves and grieves

For the incommunicant,
Whom nothing touches
And something can't.

Signs

The way a man says *Can I go in you again,*
I want to swim up you forever,
The way his hands move over your body
Like a fish, or like water moving
Over the skin of a fish,
The way he gives himself to you, sinking
Into you,
Signs that say
If there could be fish on the moon
They would gleam with a silvery light
Like his sides, they would glide
Through the blue watery heavens
Like small sleek gods,
Each carrying in its mouth
The image of
Him.

The Island of Contentment

When God was a child

I used to live on an island
Where the trees' leaves were as green as Astroturf,
And the sky was so blue you were tempted to dive heavenward.
God lived on this island too.

Often, he swam and splashed in the pool
At the base of the waterfall
While I braided reeds into baskets, bamboo
Into shades for the lean-to, weeds
And grass-blades into simple beds.

All day I worked at my weaving.
All day God swam, or plucked fish from the pool
For supper.

At night, God and I slept on our grassy beds,
He in one hut, and I in another.
The huts had no walls, and I used to hear him
Singing himself to sleep.

The tune wandered pleasantly around the island like a small breeze
While the words bobbed in the buoyant air, plump

Fruit falling from frangipani trees.

And he dreamed me,
And I dreamed him.

Green That Inspires Longings for Joy

All night, greenness lived in her mind.
It was a dream of the sea
Or bluegrass, as far as she could see.
This greenness was peaceful and kind
And magnanimous and free.

This greenness swept through her brain
And she thought, God is green
And his face, which may be seen
By the pure, while dark with pain,
Shines like a sycamore ringed with rain.

The letters of God's name are written
In green. All night she reads
A word that bleeds
Green ink. Sometimes an idea will sit in
A corner of the mind while rain beads,

On the leaded panes, like tears.
What is a dream?
If something that is not can redeem
What is real, shall we say that a dream of green that inspires
Longings for joy is only a dream?

Reading, Dreaming, Hiding

> You asked me what is the good of reading the Gospels in Greek.
> —Czeslaw Milosz, "Readings"

You were reading. I was dreaming
The color blue. The wind was hiding
In the trees and rain was streaming
Down the window, full of darkness.

Rain was dreaming in the trees. You
Were full of darkness. The wind was streaming
Down the window, the color blue.
I was reading and hiding.

The wind was full of darkness and rain
Was streaming in the trees and down the window.
The color blue was full of darkness, dreaming
In the wind and trees. I was reading you.

The Raiment We Put On

Do you remember? We were in a room
With walls as warm as anybody's breath,
And music wove us on its patterning loom,
The complicated loom of life and death.
Your hands moved over my face like small clouds.
(Rain fell into a river and sank, somewhere.)
I moved among your fingers, brushed by the small crowds
Of them, feeling myself known, everywhere,
And in that desperate country so far from here,
I heard you say my name over and over,
Your voice threading its way into my ear.
I will spend my days working to discover
The pattern and its meaning, what you meant,
What has been raveled and what has been rent.

II *Songs for a Soviet Composer*

A Text for a Musical Cycle

By the rivers of Babylon, there we sat down, yea, we wept, when we remembered Zion.

We hanged our harps upon the willows in the midst thereof.

For there they that carried us away captive required of us a song; and they that wasted us required of us mirth, saying, Sing us one of the songs of Zion.

How shall we sing the Lord's song in a strange land?

—Psalm 137:1–4

Themes

God is dead, having been stuffed into an oven
like meat. God is dead, having been eaten.
Blood is what we batten on. Therefore, love is lying,
light is scattered like bread crumbs at the creek's edge,
and free will is the reflection of time's wings in water.
My heart is shattered in the pebbled shallows and lost in the sedge.
People are dying.

Air on Air

I breathe because you do: air is love,
then, and life's like kissing oxygen.
When I sigh I touch your skin.
The breeze that sings in my lungs
may once have been your breath,
blown across an ocean.
Only that you live rescues me from death.

Song of Remembering

I meet you in my mind,
wandering among the cold-swept spaces.
Some faces are forgotten, but never yours.
I have kept you out of harm's way, in old, distant places,
where sleet still spatters a windowpane, the dead are buried in ice,
and a church spire pierces memory traces
as a needle, a vein.

Song About Being Without Him

I'm flensed like a seal, peeled
like an orange; my skin's been cut away
and spread out in the sun in lappets.
All day, dogs gnaw at my bones.
My nerves sing, strung out in the slowly vanishing light.
It grows cold. I shiver. Night rolls into my skull
like fog into an open field.

Song of Despair

I dream that you dream
of kissing me. Your mouth fastens on mine
like a fly on flypaper; my throat vaults under your hands
like a stream over rock; my back's hot and insubstantial as steam
from a pot on the stove. After supper, I latch the door.
Light leaks out of the sky. Night, like space, will sunder the south
from the far north, and leave me missing you as before.

Lullaby

I take refuge in his brain; here,
I'm safe from my own thoughts, sane

as an infant. . . . I sleep in his skull,
all my dark fears hushed by a little lullaby.

On the roof, his tears are rain.

Body Song

Put your mouth on mine
and make music with my windpipe:
my throat is a thirsty flute only sound can slake.

Each heartbeat is a note: draw your art from my body like blood,
teach spine and sinew song,
and play me all night long.

Song of the Threat

Lick the sweat from my legs,
the dew from my chin. Here's a mouthful of tears,
hot as you. Coming in,
you'll feel the earth spin out from under,
thunder will echo in the hidden cave,
and nothing will save you from getting so drunk on my slick,
    wet skin
that even the rooted tree will reel.

Aubade

Day breaks; I have cut myself on a piece of light,
and bleed dew. . . . You rise like mist from the dark ground,
spreading everywhere; you are drawn into air, released as rain.

Dawn is a word for pain and need; the vein in my wrist feeds
    weeds
as earth turns round, forsaking night.
One who wakes discovers her dream slain, her sky not blue.

Song for Two Nations

He is my one beloved country,
nonpartisan as grass. Here, I am free
as air to travel everywhere and see the sights.

At dawn the real world pulls up in a patrol car,
spits gravel and asks for me.
My lids lock against light's loud knock.

Song of the Dreaming Geologist

When I sleep, the world contracts,
like sheet metal on a cold day.
France collides with the Carolinas' red clay,
and land tracts crumple in earthquake, curled like a snail's shell.
And more: heaven is hurled into hell,
where my body's heat melts Siberia and smelts snow like ore.
When I wake, I weep.

Song of the Farmer

I plant tears
in the ground and rain shoots up.
I plant light, and pull night up by its roots.
I can't store so much grain!—It burns like a star in the sun,
while far off, the sound of his heart's starvation
is like dry thunder
pitched high above the Steppes.

Song of the Housewife

I strip the sheets from my bed
and the map from my world, bleach Red China
white. My clothes flap like Russian crows on the line
all night. Boundaries are piled like clothespins in my lap.
Each thought is a trip—but no one knows
where my garden grows. I clip slips of nations, grafting
your name onto my wild rose.

Song of Need and Desolation

Not finding him in the house, I die.
Like an astronomer, I search the sky.
Our solitary moon moves through its impassive phases,
peeling light from the birch like strips of bark.
Silence slides along the pews of an empty church; it drips from
    the dark font.
All night I die, looking for him.
My arms, my legs are becoming dead; my heart is stopped.

Song for One World

Intricate tapestry, our planet shines,
hanging its cool colors in space. Green shades into blue,
blue becomes water and fills up my cup. My table is a lake, I eat
    grass,
and carp leap onto my plate. . . . Night is a neap tide, flooding
    the forest floor,
not deep but wide. I hide in the tops of pines from dark's dull
    roar.
A new place, this steeple, undrowned, light as granite and
    graceful as the quiet hills,
where people are friends, bound by wind's wild weave.

Song About Creation

Trees are the clear bass line;
their leaves, the complication.
Deer are grace notes.
And so forth, if I define creation
as bringing into view what was previously only heard,
God's word.
On the seventh day, he listened to a little night music.

Song of the Wonderful Surprise

Start with the fact of space; fill it up
with snow. There will be snow in the sky,
snow on the ground, snow in the mysterious courtyards.
You taste snow's tang, smell snow, feel snow on your face.
If you walk forever, you will not come to a place with no snow,
but one day, looking around, you will find
a green apple hanging from a spray of snow.

Song of the Siberian Shaman

At fifty below, I slip out of my skin.
My spirit's the shadow of snow; it blows and drifts; it lies across
    the frozen field
like a fallen log; it glows like blue ice in the cracks of cliffs.
I'm thin as wind, strong as water. I peel back layers of rock,
kneel in the land's hand, rise. . . . An owl is an omen;
I eat owl meat and grow wise, discovering that what I lack
    lifts me,
like ritual feathers torn from a bird's body and dispersed among
    the dark skies.

Song of Giving

I open myself and carefully remove my heart and give it to you.
I scrape out my skull and serve up the brain cells like caviar.
I break my bones like bread, am emptied like a cup.

When I sing, sound spills from my throat like blood
from a vein; it pours into the air, and the sky turns red.
Take, eat, drink; this is my body, bled.

Song About the Second Creation

Like a stone, sound drops
into being; the waters part,
the waters close; the waves fan out, unfurled.
This is the second creation—not the bone's bright light
that starts and stops, having merely beckoned,
but the one eternity echoes,
love—the sung word flung into the world by God's loud hand.

Song of Time

The years roll down,
like a cataract over rocks.
I wade in shade; the past is a dappled glade.
Time evaporates my tears, and sun—oh, then sun
lights on my shoulder like a bird on a mulberry bush.

Nights, I sleep on wet ground, dreaming the word made flesh.

Appoggiatura

Lover, beloved, hoped-for one, listen:
Away from you, I'm as pale as the moon by day, a winter afternoon.
Antlers glisten in the dying light—deer draw near. I curl up like a
     snail,
or like drying leaves, lying on the riverbank, my ear to the earth,
     eavesdropping.
Rock's heart beats, gravity sighs; my breath knocks against cold
     clay; I hear death
keeping time until at last the land lies mute. There's sand in my
     eyes, salt in my tears.
I make shale my pillow, sleeping, having hanged my harp upon the
     willow, weeping.

Song with Footnote

Sighing, I puff my soul
into his mouth; the tip of his tongue
is like a blade, and cuts me to the quick.
I lick salt from his lips while he sips tears,
thirsty as a Cossack after a raid. One of us is crying.

This song was not sung.

Song Prophesying Happiness

First, I'll kiss his hands.
When he touches my forehead, the tormenting thoughts will fly
     from it
like the larks of Latvia in spring.
I'll let him picnic in my body as in a private park.
He'll kiss my hands,
and when I touch his forehead, the torment there will take wing.
Then we'll sing.

III *Plainsongs*

The death-list like a river flows
Down the pale sheet,
And there the whelming waters meet.
—Melville, "Donelson"

. . . try to think, at the same moment,
Of the living and the dead.
—Robert Penn Warren, "Glimpses of Seasons"

Berlin: An Epithalamion

In Berlin,
I lived in an attic, crawling
through a space barely big
enough, while
the men below drank
tea and ate hard rolls, arguing
economics. In Warsaw, snow
covered the abandoned tables
like white linen, and my boyfriend's sword on the wall
gleamed like a mounted fish. In Riga,
my boyfriend smoked
French cigarettes and promised
to marry me
and I believed him.
Snow fell in a scattered field
on the dark expanse of his leather jacket
like shrapnel.
I imagined him exploding
inside my body
like a grenade and when I pushed
his head between my legs I felt
I was getting ready to die.
There were people watching us—
there always are,
in cities like those.
Informants, blackmailers—one gets used to them.
In the morning,
he was always gone.
I would watch the sickeningly bright sun banishing the snow
    from the sill,
the glittery January icicles, no backbone, surrendering,
and turn on my side,
thinking *What will they do to us*
but I already knew the worst
thing they could do
would be nothing. I am

telling you all this
because I want you to
know that even though
love happens over
and over, riddling
our bodies until we are
scarred beyond recognition,
faceless,
and frozen,
I have chosen you
and only you
over all.

Memory

These great trees, like towering sad angels,
Feathery arms flung outward and down in a stasis of despair.
This stillness of spruces.
This silence.

Like death. Like the enormous absence
That is history, a chronology
That contradicts itself.

Yes, that's right. And just think of the ones you have
Forgotten, the substitute teacher
In fourth grade, the friend who was briefly yours
Before you betrayed her, or she you.

And the one, that man,
You went walking with,
In woods outside Riga,
The green cloud of trees
In the distance, unmoving,
Embalmed in memory, if remembered at all.

If not, he was never there.
You were never in that complicated country.
You never saw how the light persevered,
Braving its way through massed branches of spruce, birch,
    and pine
To shine like a lantern, showing

The long way back.

Looking Back

After the revolution

There was this sense of history having out-ironicized
their own ironic sense of it,
a sense of having been somehow betrayed
now that everything they had struggled against for so long
had surrendered, pliant, willing,
good-natured even,
saying *You were right, we*
were wrong,
leaving them victorious and empty-handed,
deprived of their anger.
A cold, hard rain drenched the white metal patio furniture,
and wind swept the abandoned garden.
Brightening in the strange sheen of rain light,
the stone planters squatted, secretive
as household gods,
and the terrified day hurled itself against all the other days
that had preceded it,
like a bird flying into a windowpane
it does not see is there, thinks air.
Already an invisible barrier permanently divided the past
as it had been
from what it was now
seen to have been, blood
mixing with water at the base of the glass.

History

It is what, to tell the truth, you sometimes feel
That you have had enough of, though of course
You do not really mean that, since you recall
It well enough to know things could be worse
And probably are going to get that way,
But still want a long and memorable life, which means
Having to learn more of it day by day,
The names and dates of all the kings and queens
And those less famous who ruled the territory
Known as your heart and now are gone, by one
Dark route or another, from the plot of your story.
But you write on, and are your own best Gibbon,
        And read on, this monumental subject being
        The decline and fall of almost everything.

At a Russian Writers' Colony

Alive and burning to the end.
—Pasternak, "It Is Not Seemly"

In all these rooms, the Russians write
their verses, satires, monographs.
A toilet flushes. Distant dogs bark
to one another. Someone laughs—

at the satire! Another someone coughs.
They smoke too much, these Russian writers.
They hack their way through manuscripts
with cigarettes and cigarette lighters.

Their lungs are black as Stalin's moods,
as if a fire, burning the written records
of seventy years, swept through these rooms,
this crematorium of words.

Peredelkino, 1990

Family Life in the Twentieth Century

The men go off to war
and come back with the parts of their bodies
screaming like parts of speech.
Leg! Arm! Testicle! Brain!
Their cries are like mortar fire
shelling the cities,
the turning women, restless beside them,
whose dreams are like villages
burning, burning, burning.

The Promise

We thought it had been broken.
In any case, we were sick
Of interminable speeches spoken
By leaders with two faces.
Let them eat feces,

We muttered to ourselves, returning
To our homes. Meanwhile, an army of clouds had begun to mass
Overhead, clouds that rained fire. By the next day, our homes
were burning.
Then we lived among ash and rubble.
God's face, too, we thought, was double

And death would come, despite
All assurances otherwise,
But at last we saw a kind of light,
Or many lights: a rainbow. Not like the one after the flood.
A rainbow of blood.

Report from an Unnamed City

In the square in the center of our city, there flows
unstoppingly a fountain of despair
from which we drink, hoping in this simple way to
acquire immunity to hope, for
hope is the knife that separates us from ourselves.

At night, we gather in small groups
in small, locked houses. Rain ticks against the windowpanes.
A fugitive moon slips from cloud to cloud,
seeking cover. We are still alive,
thank God. Our neighbors have been less lucky—

wiped out, like an insect colony.

Passing People on the Street

To think of where their lives will bring them is
to be without breath of your own, for that
thought will take it from you, leaving you gasping
for air. The young man with his arm around
the girl who looks at him as if he were
a walking god will one day lie in bed
catheterized. And she will see her face
in a plate glass window, and wonder who she is,
this woman uninhabited by love,
living alone on the past's small pension.

                                      And you
will be an old fool, wanting to rush in
to save them, as the buildings of their bodies
topple into dust—ruins, long forgotten
temples of a city of the dead.

In the End

In the end, light gives up the ghost
And atoms swarm, like locusts,
Over the fields of sky,
Over the highway.

In the end, the air contains
Itself, becomes its own jar and lid,
And the stars
Are suffocated.

In the end, the air seamlessly seals shut
Its own bright rifts, and all that was
Becomes indistinguishable
From all that was not.

And the blacktop thruway
Nowhere to nowhere,
And the planet like a Chevrolet
Spinning its wheels—

Time
Takes up its post at the lonely checkpoint
By the ditch,
Keeping watch.

There is nothing
But empty highway,
The cicadas chirring,
Goldenrod heavy with heat, stubborn, sweating olive trees.

In the end, there is nothing
But a uselessly beautiful planet
Wheeling among the stars
Like a Chevy Impala.

Now the Night

The air loud as an imprecation
And the wind like a fist
In the face, God himself hammering
The rain in like nails,
And who won't hang on,
Hang on for dear life?
Something we've done,
Something we've done wrong,
The grass flattened, and rain
Fleeing into the ditch
By the side of the road.
Now the brief flare of light before nightfall,
Sudden as revelation.
Now the night.

IV *A Joyful Noise*

There is nothing that God hath established in a constant
course of nature, and which therefore is done every day, but
would seeme a Miracle, and exercise our admiration, if it
were done but once.
  —John Donne, *LXXX Sermons*, No. XXII, Easter Day,
    March 25, 1627

O wonderful, wonderful, and most wonderful, wonderful!
and yet again wonderful, and after that, out of all whooping!
        —Shakespeare, *As You Like It*, Act III, scene ii

Grammaire Générale: A Review

The study of the universal conditions that prescribe the form of any
human language is "grammaire générale." Such universal conditions
. . . provide the organizing principles that make language learning
possible. . . . By attributing such principles to the mind, as an innate
property, it becomes possible to account for the quite obvious fact that
the speaker of a language knows a great deal that he has not learned.
                    —Noam Chomsky, *Cartesian Linguistics*

(for J. F.)

Ten years later, I still remember the way
Your mouth on mine could make me say
Words I didn't know I knew.
Even my legs learned a new
Language. Then, speaking in tongues, I spoke with my tongue.
(I could have parsed you all night long.)

Thus love is a predicate, making sense
Of its subject even in the past tense.
Thus we conjugated, and our parts
Of speech burst into song,
As did our innocent hearts.
(I could have parsed you all night long.)

I remember how your hand translated time
Into eternity. Alas, what scans won't always rhyme:
Between *a priori* and *ex post facto*, language
Falls silent, and lovers age.
I remember what we said when we were young.
(I could have parsed you all night long.)

Love is a verb, bringing one object to bear
Upon another. It modifies fear.
Lord, we were brave and gerundive, giving
Ourselves to each other. Language is for the living;
Love is a diphthong.
(I could have parsed you all night long.)

43

Ten years later, I remember your mouth
On mine, its sweetness inflected with the South.
Fluent in love, you affixed your root to my prefix.
(We used adverbs for kicks.)
That night, we taught each other what we'd known all along.
(And I could have parsed you all night long.)

That night, words became hands and held each other.
Words became bodies and whispered touches, conversing
    with collar-
Bone, elbow and knee. Love is the mother
Tongue; you were a born scholar
And you taught me all the right ways to go wrong.
(And your dangling participle was so well hung.)

(I could have parsed you all night long.)

The Name

You were shocked when you heard it,
Self-reflexive as an act of self-love,
Spelling itself in an alphabet of fire,

And you were ashamed and confused: you had been given this
    secret
To tell, but you could not tell it without revealing to the world
Your irrepressible pride in yourself, your joy at finding yourself

Even here, in the wilderness of history,
Because it was your name too: I AM.

Woman Living Alone

A book on the bed,
radio turned to a classical station.

Raining or not raining, but if it is, the water rushes
into the bushes by the side of the brick house,

bridal wreath bushes, their white flowers
like snow in spring.

If it is not raining,
there may be a blue sky like a blessing

being pronounced over a meal, which,
though taken alone,

tastes of life.

Love

In the attention it pays to each detail,
In its frailty and flexibility,
In the way it seeks out a new trail
While stumbling repeatedly upon the old,

You will know love, and know
That what it cannot fail to do
Is render even this late scene
In all its abundance,

The red-tailed hawk overhead,
Spongy moss springing from wet bark,
The sound of your own walking
Through these autumnal woods.

Work

The old dog, Work, one eye blind as if seeing
wore it out, a limp in his hindquarters,
lies on his stomach on the floor at your slippered feet,
content merely to dream in your presence.

In his old age, the fur on his paws has grown
so long he, too, seems to have on slippers.
When you reach down to rub his wary ears,
he sends you a secret message of gratitude.

Strange to be here so idly, after the days
of long walks, of chasing squirrels and sticks.
The days of hunting down reluctant quarry.
There were many days when he was your one companion.

It is you who should thank him, and so you do,
inwardly. His eyes as they look up at you
are unspoken words; the blind one surely says
love. He rests his muzzle on his paws.

It may snow tonight. The storm windows
muffle the racket of the semis as they speed
past your house toward Illinois; the fire in
the fireplace makes a warm spot on the dog's coat,

you are warmed by both the fire and your dog
while candles burn and the coffee kettle heats.
It is as if your whole house is on fire
with a fire that does not burn or hurt.

This is home, where you and your old dog, Work,
hang out together, especially in autumn,
when the late tomatoes are killed by frost
and smoke from your chimney spirals into night.

Evensong

The summer day unfolds its wings
　　Like time flying.
All day, bright light sings like a swan,
　　Dying.

Light floats down from the sky, light
　　As a feather.
It drifts toward night
　　And a change of weather.

The sun sets suddenly, burning
　　Bridges, the blaze rising higher
And higher over the earth's methodical turning.
　　Night puts out the fire.

All things cool and harden, after being singed.
　　Day gives way to night.
The song the white swan sang,
　　Day sings tonight.

In the silence that ensues, all things
　　Close up; night
Snuggles its head in its protective wings
　　All night.

The living room lights blink on, then off.
　　People and pets all sleep.
Time that flew, now sinks
　　Into the laky deep.

All sleep.

Grace

You know of course that you haven't earned it.
For if you had, it would not be what it is:
Beauty of the candle after you've burned it,
The dark bird rising like smoke, always from ashes,
Remembrance of heat and light, describing itself
Invisibly upon the air of the mind,
That takes the life lived in a fury of self-
Love and remakes it into something that shined
So brightly that it might have been a star,
Instead of the candle you were burning at both ends.
And now the night grows black, wherever you are,
Except for the golden shimmer that descends
To the earth through miles of lonely outer space
And lights up your misspent life, with saving grace.

Redemption

Into darkness, out of light
   I plunged. Breathy in midflight,
     I lost sight

of all below—
   there was no
     bright crescendo

of sea, nor the slower
   movement of a sycamore
     growing tall, or even the lower

life forms' Darwinian crawl.
   Everything had stopped but my noisy fall,
     uncorrectable,

at the start of which my side,
   still cleaving to God's tough hide,
     had torn—wide

open! The gap in my body
   whistled as I fell down the starry
     chute, and the C-

sharp music of my deficiency
   was a symphony.
     Thus we become what we cannot be.

Out of darkness, into light I go,
   I go, discarding the useless cargo
     of myself. I rise, I am so
       light.

And Then

And then a vast, surprising peacefulness
descended, like a blue shadow upon
the snow; and the shadow sleeping on the snow
was a kind of reconciliation, form
embraced by content, light by light, the birds
hanging from the branches like bright red berries.

And then for days, there was nothing to disturb
the beauty of that equilibrium,
which was so like the miracle of forgiveness.

Waiting for the End of Time

Behind the window, in that room where rain
And wind were instrumentalists playing
On the windowpane, you were asleep, again,
And never heard the words that I was saying.
I didn't say them for you to hear, I said
Them to your heart, that listening, third ear.

What anyone's heart knows is what has been bled
Out of it. . . .

       It's February, a different year,
And spring seems something that a season might do
For the sheer delight of being sprung,
A kind of rhythm, a heartbeat, or *parlando*
(The words are spoken even though they're sung),
And everything is different now, except
Time itself, which goes right on being kept.

The Heart of the World

> Each thing in the world has a heart and the world in its entirety
> also has a heart.
>
> —Rabbi Nachman of Bratzlav

When the clouds gamboled over the blue pasture of sky like newborn lambs patiently licked and smartly nudged by their mother the wind, and cardinals blossomed like red roses on the long trellis of the horizon, and the mountain, still patched with winter white, was like a great cow, say a great cow mooing far off, a sound like separation, plaintive, certainly, and yet expectant because even a cow believes, even if it does not know it believes, that in spite of everything reunion just because it is right must also be possible, the heart of the world, which lives in every living thing and is more easily broken even than the commandments of the Lord our God, which, saith the sages of old, number six hundred thirteen, skipped   a beat.

Narcissus "Galilea"

For Frannie, a CPA, who gave them to me

This gift wrapped in the thin white paper of itself:
the paper-whites have green shoots now,
tongues of green fire.

Each bulb is a church with a spire
shooting for the sky.

Narcissi bear white blossoms like little clouds
that drift higher and higher, a Dow

that never falls, the ransom
that buys the world back from

death, the deliverer, the greenest thumb.

Prayer

May night, when it comes, be merely lack of light,
the stars unbright in a blue-black sky
that is the visual analogue of a sigh—

God's sigh, expressing love and sadness,

and the faintest note of amused exasperation
sounded at the edge of the universe
like a quasar, or the rhyme at the end of a verse.

God's Friends Will Wear Rain*bows

Blessed are those who wash their robes.
—Revelation 22:14

This is a poem about God
And about those who are "robed in the long friends"
(A bow to Dylan Thomas, the old friend who said that), or in
   other words, dead, their once-strong will
To live slugged by accident or exhaustion's fist into senselessness,
   knocked across this space of time into the kingdom where
The power and the glory are God's, and his reign
Is supreme, and in his presence, even an egalitarian bows.

In God's kingdom, the leaves that are falling from golden boughs
(Frazer, of course) heal the nations (Revelation 22:2) upon which
   they fall. On the right hand of God
And on his left hand, sheltering among the trees from the cool
   rain,
Sit (like Buddha and Jesus) all those who are robed in the long
   friends,
That mysterious metaphorical covering which they wear
And which shines like light and which we will

Put on ourselves one day. There is, here, no question of free will
(Calvin). Drawing our spangled robes around us, pinning starry
   bows
In our hair, we will enter the kingdom of God, wearing
What one wears in the presence of God:
Friends.
Take care that your robes of long friends do not shrink in the
   heavenly rain.

Under trees or eaves, even the dead must come in out of the rain,
Which, in heaven, appears to fall like golden spears (Blake)
   and will,
If you are not careful, rend your friends
Into tatters, strips, scraps, mere ribbons and bows.

When you present yourself to God,
You will want to wear

Your best outfit and look your best. God may be everywhere,
But the kingdom of God, where God reigns,
Is not, and when you go there and first meet God,
It is only natural, indeed inevitable, for there is no question of
    free will
(Augustine) here, that you will want to arraign yourself, before
    the throne under those watery boughs,
Robed in your best friends.

Therefore, all your life, take good care of your friends.
Do not wear them casually or everywhere.
When rain falls, catching you under black leafless boughs
(Ezra Pound, Li Po) glistening with the delicate light that hides
    in little drops of rain,
Remember that it will
Not be long before you meet God.

On that sad or splendid day, your friends will
Say that you have gone to be with God, where
Eternity is the unbroken arc, cast across the inbound universe,
    of a rainbow.